T0114960

FATE AND FAITH
POEMS

Kraftgriots

Also in the series (POETRY)

FATE AND FAITH
POEMS

Tunde Adeniran

kraftgriots

Published by
Kraft Books Limited
6A Polytechnic Road, Sango, Ibadan
Box 22084, University of Ibadan Post Office
Ibadan, Oyo State, Nigeria
✆ + 234 (0)803 348 2474, + 234 (0)805 129 1191
E-mail: kraftbooks@yahoo.com
kraftbookslimited@gmail.com
www.kraftbookslimited.com

First published 2015

ISBN 978–978–918–326–5

= KRAFTGRIOTS =
(A literary imprint of Kraft Books Limited)

First printing, September 2015

Dedication

To: GOD ALMIGHTY

"For from him and through him and to him are all
things"

And

For: CHRISTOPHER OKIGBO

&

WOLE SOYINKA

"Quicquid erit, erit"

Preface

Ever willing to take a flight on the mystery of imagination, I took time off to commune with the mythological world of the fairy. I returned with nothing. Nothing but jottings of the language of the spirit that left me puzzled about my mission! My soul kept talking to itself about the blessings that some burden had swept to the sandy shore of life.

Once again I saw myself refusing to cling to my code. I was with an expanding range of subject matter, in thought and action covering contemporary issues and eternal verities. Since I have always had hope and continue to dream about fate and faith but without any intimidating sentries to guard and defend our common values, mores, cosmos and humanity at life's warfront beyond the written word, I have chosen to join others in throwing some rays on the cloud around us.

The art of exploring the unknown and searching one's heart is a life-long preoccupation. Poetry being a discipline of meditation and craft, however, conveying one's state of mind could be through what has been said before – for effect, emphasis or instrumental reiteration. This is the essence of including in this volume some of the poems previously published under the titles **Fate Unearthed** and **Apropos of Faith.** It is my hope that the present generation will move from lamentation to action, restore hope and actualize potentials and promises betrayed. With faith, the manifestation of truth and justice may yet become a legacy of the future.

Tunde Adeniran
July, 2015

Contents

Testimonies

Ìbà

Ìbà ooo ìbà
ÌbàOlú-Òrun my creator
I woke up in wonderment
of His wonders.
His mercies unceasing
Ageless.

Ìbà ooo ìbà
To mysteries embodiment
My maker, redeemer and deliverer
from life's raging storms
the world's tempestuous seas.
The one who is all
Unfathomable.

Ìbà ooo ìbà
I rise to write
and I remember
Oluwole Akinwande Soyinka
Christopher Okigbo
Kofi Awoonor
sending messages in songs
stringent voices trumpeting
that man should lose his chains
dispense with cages and disperse
the dispensers of terror
and courtiers of destiny changers.

The majestic sail of your words
are beyond oceans.
Words fly and dance
at your command
across meadows and mountains

blowing winds and whirlwinds
over islands into inlands
causing trees to swing
and knocking down prison gates.

Ìbà ooo ìbà
for your measureless manna
to the initiates
and regular overdose
from the treasure
of waters that run deep.

When your voice explodes
no submarine could silence it
and you offer no liniment
to soothe wounded beasts
of the charged arrows
from your sharp tongues.

You sing soothing songs.
Some lyric to the lonely.
The messages of your songs
travel through echos and drums
in season after season
are heard like trumpets of war
and some like ballads of alchemy.

Lend me your voice
the ecphonesis of rage
against grief and despair
unguent for the wailings
of the weak and wasted.

With fresh and strong voices
new initiates queue in quest
painting lives and singing allegories.
I learn to cheer the parrots

that I may secure my voice
Ìbà ooo ìbà.

Ìbà ooo ìbà
to the balm of my pains
sweats dropping in many colours
painting pictures of my dreams
in the season of sunny weather
Ìbà ooo ìbà.

Africa

A movement like Cycling
in Herculean elegance
Old. Yet so new.

A Kilt for the Scot. *Marseillaise* for the French.
What is it for the African . . . the Lover
with no tongue to kiss?

Quislings at Parleys search for shelter
for shadows and the rainbow
in the desert of abandoned Oases.

Mandela the conqueror

Not one of them
birds and beasts of passage.
He came under a dark sky
drenched in the rain of hate.

Downcast thrust and hedged
hounded by the huntsmen
along paths of intemperate beasts
and birds fouling soil and soul.

They sought to share
the land, the air and the hopes;
the winds to deliver waves
of thoughts and action in collision.

He walked to still the tide
beaming light of justice, compassion
and human dignity
to the chagrin of colour vultures.

Wheezed, unbended and unbowed.
A legend runs their steam and stream dry
spreading tides for new harvests
of a new dawn and new hopes.

With the torch of emancipation
fired by imagination
with gravitas he conquered
blind warriors against the soul.

Hail mandela!

Hail Mandela
Hail Mandela.
The symbol of our past
The spirit of our future.

Hail Mandela
Hail the Madiba
who taught us to know
the many routes unknown.

The paths of thunder await
waiters on the cliff
wrestling for hangers to cling
facing downwards without a compass.

Mandela's chosen path we know
rugged not for the roller-blade
far-flung beyond the reach of fools
drumming anger to songs of envy.

Heroine of fate

How endangered the generations
in need of heroes and heroines!
And she could not look back.
She faced the future
and saved fatherland
from disasters in the wings.
Tales untold cannot immure
the testimonies of your fate.

Now Queen of our hearts
the grief of the Cardosos
Great-grand-daughter of Herbert Macauley
the nationalists' nationalist.

What if she had chickened out
retreated and ushered in
the epidemic that was Patrick Sawyer
clothed in the garment of ebola?

What if Amayo, first line of defence
of renowned genealogy
jewel of the adadevohs
had looked the other way?

What if stellar Stella
proud daughter of africa
had quaked than quarantine
In the face of virulent villainy?

What if the medical virtuoso
had despaired in confusion
confounded by solicitous envoys
loitering the gate of adversity?

The gift of August was dreadful.
May it not be Africa's eraser
like the 14th century *yersinia pestis*
with Europe's two hundred million souls gone!

Spread not the flaming EVD.
Cast away the funeral
but ignite the fire
of raw patriotism
uninfected by space and time
from Ghana's Volta region
to Lagos Island
and Nigeria's hinterland.

Kongi's harvest
(for W.S)

You are welcome
to our party of many toasts
for the lion's timely arrival
a throaty roaring across valleys
and hills for the jewel
through crypts and seasons of anomie.

The rodeo had long been scattered
the ranch ransacked and raked
by randy ranzellars –
aliens who hover and hound
the promise of our pastures
locked in the uterus of history.

We were brought in by mid-day
to busy our hoes, cutlasses and paddles
tearing through thickets and torrents
of virginlands and tempestuous rivers
unmapped, untamed but ready
for man's tilling, toiling and tunneling.

Mountains spew mines and valleys orgeat
the rivers flotilla and fishes
as the sower spreads his tentacles
on rivers and lands that sniff and swell
as the seeds of seasons sprout
sucking hard into nature's womb.

Look over the rolling rivers
across the distanced gulfs and cliffs
through the vast lowland and highplains
and view the growth and fruition

of ageless seeds of the hoeing hands
the vatic trumpeter for our greenery.

A toast for the plougher
here in this scorching sun
for the October harvest has come
in its sumptuousness and splendour
for him who sows and sings
with a lion's deep breath.

Come on here and manufacture
a laugh if not a smile
that untried stomachs may rock
and get us into some rollicking
with songs from the penguins
of flightless visions.

Welcome once again
to a harvest delayed
the championed pathfinder is crowned
enstamped and now we'll chant
and so the tippling and toasting
for this is Kongi's harvest!

The town crier
(*for Chris Okigbo*)

Dear You, Chris – The – crier

The tumultuous forest is now tranquil:
Devoid of the didactics of your thundering **DRUMS.**

But our eddied streams are forever devising
deployment of Criers against cadencies.
The silencing of **SILENCES**.

Bright again the searchlights are beaming, searching . . .
Searching at noon for rodents in the market-place
and **THUNDER** is now in repose avoiding the **LIMITS**
where caduous leaves won't fall.

How do we realize **DISTANCES?**
Demons will quarrel with darkness
for drawing the dawn to the day
trapped along the paths through **HEAVENSGATE**
into the **LABYRINTH . . .** beyond the irongate.

Heed thee: Come back unseen.
We need them echoes
from the hereafter. Messages
of your drum, the iron bell.
Ding at the gate of numen
for folks out on a limb.

The serene forest is now dentate
with ravines and rough rivers.
But onward, the sailors cry.
Wraths whine and whirr:

The WORD, the whirling wind
The WORD is the whistler where
fates fluster & flutter.

---

* Christopher Okigbo, the ***"town-crier . . . with (the) iron bell
was a meteor."***
One of the greatest poets of the 20th century, he was killed during
the Nigerian Civil War.

Saturday child

Forceful light . . . Restless might.
     Fixed foray through haggled darkness;
     wind of the dawn . . .
     envoy of daylight.
The Trinity
in whom beauty cloys. The virile
epitome of the creative soul.
In harmony with sounds . . . pitched
     against the nefarious wind disbursing
     bundled scrimmages.

Thumbprint on the face of history.
Tipped by stars
the scale-watcher trades in fairness . . .
fairness for faith & fancy for fun.
Opal mind. Golden sheen.
The diamond of lustrous essences;
Quintessence of the veracious . . .
     You are
the golden scale of justice.

Guiding uptrend of the upwind.
God-given
     Child of the deities
     anointed of the creative essence.
Go not into the lake, dear radix:
Your Voice is in the wind
You fountain of the season's secrets.
     Moil to preserve the locus of fate . . .
earth thing for the earth.

Saturday is spring . . . the exordium of fresh life
Saturday is season of rebirth:

Saturday child –
earnest supplicant . . . steadfast giver.

Mind not the grim reaper:
Vacuous the ventures of the vamp.
Inanity when common misery is fed on common anger.
Wreak no havoc
expiate with familial fervour
in the race with time . . .
alone
at the gate of tomorrow.

Fate Unearthed

How is your messiah?

For every clan and country a Messiah
    emerges to ride

the new shadow of an old moon.

Our Messiah once saved us
    from ourselves. Daily
he delivers us from posterity and
tailors the contours
    of our destiny.

How is your Messiah?
Can he ride
        or give a ride?

Does he capture cronies and create
Croesuses . . . among constituent folks?

Does your Messiah suck saliva?
    Usury for the air you breathe . . . Is he a Confidant
    . . . or Camorrist? Callist . . . or
    Cur Manifest?

Fate

Ethereal child in the delicate womb
of the Unknown; greetings.

Before your compelling presence stand I
captive of the Karma and of god-men.

Your decrees . . . my feasance:
forever do leaves fly in praise of the gale.

Your essence divulges to them who
yield to the force of magical reliefs.

D'you say I must paddle my canoe
along these rock-strewn gullies?

Clean the candent carcass of yesterday which today
does not even belong in the casket?

So webby & sealed from chance and changes. The immortal
pathfinder for earthly quests!

Sometimes open-faced . . . occasionally furtive but
forever emblematic of nemesisian proximity.

The human heart adjures you streak
this mountain hidden with a cloud.

Fate, I beseech thee: keep signaling. The enigmatic
Amity of supremacy and being human.

The caucus

At the Caucus we dance
and sing. Our steps and songs change daily and are heard
from Gethsemane to Golgotha
ad infinitum.

No flyleaf salute today, Counselor
We know you need no lantern
to see these flowered "fibres"
Carousing in the caucus court.

Again, look. Just look . . . and listen
I have but one question on the dance and songs:
why this dance again? yes
the dance of yesterday! Mere mirth?

But those on the fence are readying
for this nimb'less dance and the dry song.
Aren't we here to compose a new song . . .
perform a ritual of atonement?

There are so many whys
the searing searching soul can't understand. Or
can it understand the maddening why itself? This
fevered bathing in feverish waters?

Those crackles are urging that we leave. Quit for
the carking and genteel go-between
for caucus and country carrying
showers for a thirsty land.

What else do we need: mothering or moulting . . .
To honour the bittersweet summon? To skip
away from displacing the roots
to preserve the leaves?

Counselor, we've danced enough. Swung too much
to this song. Pull us back from these shallow jollities.
They lead to the dark abyss, through the path
carefully cursed by caucusing Cukolds.

Exotiana

Come with me
away from infernal regions.
come with me to the land
of pendent twig and leafless festoons.
the dogs here don't bark.
They drink grog and gnaw razor blades
and the forest murmurs
only when the trees do not creak.

Come with me to the real wilderness.
Explorers for here are tuned elsewhere
and only those afraid of mountains
are left with backpacks.

We store our thoughts in lathe
and pray for acarnan
for those who give here
do not receive.

Come with me to the common theatre
where millions splurge with villainy
and the man to watch
is the watchman.

An illusion?

Seeing the warrior and his world
across the windy field rising;
moving out of the self
like soldiers seized by od:
clanging
     tapping
       marching.
Sounds of horn:
hums of siege.
Thoughts locked
like winter seeds
lost in summer dreams.

Human spirit

In me and you
The hormones secreted
in pristine shells
molts . . .
        yielding
whirlwind & conundrum.

Winnowings . . .
and in the winds are gyrations:
        the regnant home
        is unsure of its essence
        carry water in a scuttle
        or wash stains
        from coloured salt?

Something in you &
in me is welt
of the thing in us –
lolloping
and marching
to the beat of drums
by something
in me . . .
and you.

This **THING** shielded
by veils unknown
by you and me
may lie hulklike
or become effluent
. . . effulgent
forceful
like lightnings flashing

34

& carrying
messages from thunder
through light and shadows.

      ****

By itself steedlike
and in ghoulish poise
suborns me and you
into elegant walks
on thorns . . .
makes the mouth smile
while the body shivers
and a badgered heart
receives from another soul
smirks.

Yet it's the amulet –
fire and water combined &
alone unconquerable by angst
since the sun that sets
also rises.

Self avoidance

You stand before the mirror
looking straight at the flat glass
moving backward and forward
left and right
and adjusting not to see
the image being reflected.

Walk away and hold
the breadth of your feelings.
Walk back and view
the blessings of age.
Smile . . . Smile . . . and laugh
to reveal some hideous contours.
For as you walk back
away from the mirror
at the cave
you march back into darkness.

Bread

Making bread is an art.
Breaking bread is art.
Crumb-dropping is art's art.

Porgy or papaw today
          for the carnivore?
          Send the birds away
            from the mango tree . . .
            they'll eat in the oven.

Leave the milk jar
          for the cows . . .
          they'll feed on cream.

Leave the water too . . .
          right there
on the mountain. The fishes
will have it for dinner.

The belly resounds
          in polyphonics . . .
incessant paranoid pleas . . .
          Stale crumbs
          to slake
          God-given addiction.

Meat for the dogs . . .
          What else
          for the hawks?

Who ate yesterday?
Who will eat
& drink today . . .
and tomorrow?

Johny's paycheque

Hundred pounds
Hundred pounds.
Hundred pounds
from all the grimace.

Hundred pounds.
for a stew of bruises.

Hundred pounds
Hundred pounds.
Hundred pounds
from the sweat of brawn.

Hundred pounds.
from the yield of yells.

Hundred pounds
Hundred pounds.

The landlord will come
and twenty will go.

The headmaster will call
and twenty he'll get.

The tax collector will scoop
and thirty must go.

And the family must live
but is thirty for all that matter?

To their source
Hundred pounds are gone.

Hundred pounds
Hundred pounds.

Hundred pounds
for what a life?

Youth

I

peeved by the thought of spent hopes
the cornucopia of glittering visions
keeper of the unrevealed.

purr now . . . nod later. seek . . . live
like organs of pure existence. snigger not
at faults; fear the nick of nemesis.

II

Young like the wee hours of dawn
On the verge of day
Unveiled force
Timed to tune the terra
Hallowed in the lee of fate.

```
        y
     o   o
    u       u
   t        t
  h         h
```

Native wind

Abroad at home:
Native wind, when will you blow
and make your kindred grow?
When will you stop sweal'ing . . .
Swashing like curbless swirls?
Breeze is not for him who swagger
for the sleight to sup the sudor
of estranged kith and kin
The cloudy sky is in retreat
refusing to yield rain.
What tidings native wind?

Anamnesis

Unardoned . . . Iam the larva.
Hoodwinked. And mangled
by moping gales
of stability.
But won't the Larva assume the Pupa?
Won't Chrysalis liberate me, the self . . .
shackled in the cocoon
of alien valley?

Dual ways

Dual ways
of dual carriages
dual views, dual visions.

Destiny and Fate
in dual forms . . .
part of dual hopes

Dual means are measured
by dual powers
expressed in dual ways.

Mors voluntaria: A poem on suicide

Each one after the other
the skinny and the fat
tall or short
in turns they sank
deeply
into heaven's trough.

The Panga sieves
the tortoise from its shell.
It devours in early mornings
in late afternoons . . .
and in the quiet darkness of night
along open byways.

The Cyclone disjects
the shepherd from his flock
and preys.

The dry face of the atomizer
sucks and ravens.
It shatters.

Seven pots of palm oil for Èsù
But what's for them –
rat breeders who hire cats
for babysitting?
What's for them who despise fruits
and quest for buds?

Entreat Ògún with libations
at noon and at night
by the road side
where the vipers lay
drinking blood
and crunching bones.

I smell blood

I smell blood,
Cold blood.

I smell blood on earth:
in the mountains,
the oracles are dumb.
On the seas,
the miracle birds are dozing.

I smell blood in the air:
in the thin air.
Spooks of salient statures . . .
these elements everywhere
claim to be nowhere

Ambushed Rabbi performs Papal mass.

I smell blood:
The culver invests in incendiaries
Gilded blood of angels stain the sky.
I smell blood
In changeless forms.

I smell blood
on the farm:
The fading of fiefs,
deaths deadening the dead
I smell blood.

I smell blood.
Irascibility incarnate.

I smell blood where
Sleep sleeps in sleep.

and sleep will not soothe
the weary eyes.
I smell blood.

I smell blood
amidst picnics & panics –
The arrival of didymous,
the knave and the diddler are wedded
like flora and fauna.

The snail presides over a feast of salt.

I smell blood
Waif wangles way to the wharf
the imp refuses to tuck his dagger
and thinking is a waste of thought.
I smell blood.

I smell blood
on a lonely road:
Vultures spit unannealed
Myrmidon & mammon cuddle erinys
supreme cloudiness in the sky.

I smell blood,
Cold blood.

Guardian of the stars

The owl hoots
as darkness
     in tidelike pageantry
wave stars
into the womb of night
     through the open gate
      entrusted to the guardian
      who drops off
      as the owl toots.

But the guardian lingers
     in seclusion:
contemplating the glow,
the tint & the peace
which departed
     with the stars
and desiring raindrops
to chastise the earth
     for letting loose the stars . . .
or some alleys
     in which to await
     another day
     and lie amidst the earthbound
     sucking warmth
     from the sun.

Vampires

Songs came cadenced
and tuneful. allegretto
drumbeats lure
the young
and the old rushed
for a welcome
but are seized
by the chill and kisses
of lamias.

Thought you were gone
for good. Thought the pang
of succubus shall never
here again be felt.

But now some hidden
restive hands
will go
and come again
creating ripples
in static lakes,
hewing bodies
young and old.

They'll come daring
in defiance of pandects
and go deaddrunk
now and forever
leaving behind a people
in search of eunomy
and soul.

Born to die

Down there in the meadow.
In the socket of a shadeless valley
lies a baby boo-hooing
and fingerwebbingin the air.

He's oppilated
from sighting the surrounding awnings
by smoke. His haunch bruised,
the child lies in repose.

The lake beneath the valley
is almost dry and devoid of fish
but loons loom and are guided
by harpies and the cacus.

Screams . . .
but no tousing yet.
Echoes of laughter
all around the valley.

No farewell

(For Rev. Sam. Oluremi Aina who lives in death)

Colourful shadows, lethal delusions
the twilight between elfish visitation & the departure
of a strategic star in the wee
hours of meteoric losses.

Whistled wailings vault into trembling
whimperings. Melting grief. Gloom
and flowing tears lament the fate
against which deities and gnomes never warned.

Once the roarless but unmastered lion:
too peppered for the imp
and the nymph. The boiling water
for the priested fires. Now the manacled!

Hopes fingered . . . wrenched. Mother earth
tittered over bowing flowers, fronds and eternal grief.
Stillness there. Coldness here.
Secreted fluids again the bier had sucked.

To the ghost-hands & muted schemers, no victory!
Look into your garden . . . the Vrita-ravaged vineyard where
the clock had ceased its chiming
and realize what you've lost.

Oluremi: for you these wreaths. Hallowed dirge
over your tomb. In you the sun set at noon but
your spirit **LIVES** . . .
No Farewell.

If only . . .

(A poem for the African woman and for mother Earth)

I

I've heard your voice in many tones
Your face conjours fire and water
Your voice the lyric of my breath.

I've seen your blood move and squall
I've felt the rubblings in my veins resounding
the whispers of the African wind.

I've watched you swing and dance
Hands raised to the melody of trumpets
to sounds of unseen drums

I've known your moments of joy
Your thoughts pace to and fro
they keep searching on.

I've seen you trot and frisk
in the brisk of early morning
in the tender moments of life's innocence.

I've got to yearn and skip
before the music here
fades to a diminuendo.

II

If only echoes could come
before the voices
from inlands to islands
sending messages across the seas.

If only solipcists could know
that the exit from the path
of loneliness is close . . .
a little farther from uncommon routes.

If only hunters could hear
the ironic grin of the rain god
which rejects late propitiation . . .
poor libations for pure alchemies

If only Oya could feel
the chill and swill of late floods;
if she could hear
of sango's anxious sentinels.

Your face now mother as I lay
clothed in night's roomy darkness
remembering only those dreams
i never dreamt.

Subdued vibrations

Like children awaiting magic
we're watching a pond half-filled
with silenced fishes.

. . . gyrations without impulses
      Of them whose hands and legs are tied
      For the acrobat in the King's courtyard.
silence and silence
all faces at the sky awaiting
what Peter promised.

Seaside seances

Spellbound to will
the spirits of conatus
march along
Zodiacal feats
    smelling feaces
      thinking they're fodders
    hearing dirges
      sounding like sonatas
     seeing the dead dining
      but disbelieving
     touching ghosts
       and feeling no can-trips
     tasting acids & taking
      aldose for money.

And fishes picnicking on sand?

Meditation at the tomb

Solemn warblings
along a path untrodden &
unknown.
Moments of hallucinations.

Mandolin in hand
I am seated
between tranquil rivulets
and squalling elms
within the quoins
of the fathomless.

Ears are stiff
hands are paralyzed.
No fire here
to dry the freezing body
congealed in a cave.

Chthonic Moros*
taciturned in the silent
underground vault
with the shards and shadows of jàkùnmò**
open forth now
the kernel.

I'll keep looking
at the pregnant sky
if it may hold on
since I have a voice
and I have my wand.
Maybe I can give
a music different
from the murmurs

of maenads in mucks.

Maybe from my music
will stillness submit to movement
in the tomb of shadows where
everything hunts but
nothing sees
nothing feels
and everything is nothing.

---

* Moros (the personification of fate) is the mythical child of Nyx, an ancient Greek goddess embodying the essence of night (and whose mythical stature could be equated with that of Nox-the ancient Roman goddess personifying night).

** An "enemy" of daylight, Jàkùnmò – a night (mythical) wanderer – is regarded by the Yoruba as an impish satellite of the god of night and darkness.

Take me, rhythm!

take me down across the valleys
take me beyond the lakes of gore
hold my arm beyond the ankle
move my legs with the strength of dreams.

motion of life still i stand
lead my eyes with smiles of hope
above the leaves that dry and drop
beyond the mornings of moaning and mourning.

close in fast on the distance ungauged
poke and stir the leery pilgrim
before the moon and vespers come take me
take me rhythm before the sun withdraws!

Dance

Dance . . .
this dance.
I love to dance;
wriggle my wrists and waists
and let out sweats
of fear and folly.

Dance . . .
let's dance
to the victors' tune;
it's the tune of Concience,
of truth and freedom
in crowded parties.

Dance . . .
with this dance
of anxiety and hope
we'll outdance ravaging dances
of those fires and funerals
of them steamed & stained.

Beirut-ulster and soweto

They darkened the house
to fake the return of darkness.

For how long will the spirit smoulder
under canopies of alien fires?

What will happen when
no more temples to break
no more rubbles to shatter
no more ruins to bury
no more weaklings to pluck
and the souls in blanket
fly over the ocean of tears
the sea of blood and the charnels
and undaunted they rise . . .
thrust inviolate and demand a price
from those who estrange the soul
from the body and sustain alien avatar
with powder and native blood.

Who are the children of Sisyphus
playing the tambourine of terror?
Who turned Beirut-Ulster red
and rendered Soweto lightness?
Who served sweetened sand with sanicle
and called for a wedding
of life and death?

Heroes without a cause

Faces kindle. Eyes flake.
They stumble down
rollicking and roaring
toward deserted city gates
with bucolic joys
for having witnessed it all.

Who dare blow pan-pipes
for soggy-selves
but drunken mortals?
Who'll offer kisses
to a land painted in blood
but the lost whose boom is doomed?

Across from the gateways lies a court
guarded with eyes unblinking . . .
with faces spreading the message of fire
while bowed heads refuel cleansing-fires
in the corridors where they'll learn
how to spell D-E-F-E-A-T.

No thanks to the babylifters

The flights had been spontaneous
like night-birds in retreat
along Asian valley lanes.
And sometimes sporadic like the gaits
of anxious but weary horses
led astray by the heave of their riders.

They slip one after the other
pulsating and sprawling in blood and yet departing
into sinking ships
as fire is set on homes
while adventurers search for flames
to shade their own shadows.

Head or tail?
Who will breathe in the dark
of a shelter whose light is gone?
The men must be back in the trenches
and for the women refugee camps will suffice
but the kids shall go as orphans.

Bodies move and are shooed at airports.
Sprouting souls cling to flesh
that refuse to bear children.
Blood-soaked pitying hands squeeze and pat
yellow "ownerlesses" as white multitude extol
Changs and Chins becoming Jacks and Jerrys.

No thanks to you – babylifters of a lifted land
for you and I know
that this game of the foxes
is no act of the entheate
and although today lifted from his root
the "orphan" shall tomorrow root your lifts.

Walls

Walls. Walls.
separated by walls you are
so close, yet so far.

Walls, the dynamites:
walls between man & man
walls between man & himself

Walls between subsets & supersets
walls between rhetorics & actions
Walls. Walls.

Behind walls you play
Peter against Paul . . . & toss
Tantalus in torrents.

Walls dehumanize
those who create walls. Walls destroy
whoever tolerates walls' creation.

Walls between the Clergy
and the Laity. Walls are the dirk
on the heart of peace.

Walls yield walled thoughts:
forgive a foe or kill a kin?
Walls. Walls.

Of surrealism and madness

Looking deep into the cracks
in some walls
I see some movement:
Something André Breton, Freud
or Lionel Trilling
may never know . . .
Something Pound and Joyce,
Eliot and Yeats
may never feel.

Poets . . .

They may know
the paths of thunder
but not the paths
of the lizard which roams
in walls' roomy cracks
hiding
away from the festival lights
throughout the village.

Phantoms?

This image is dim . . .
fixed and unclear
behind some shadows,
some rugged hills
and lowly places
surround a crowd of men
in stupor.

And I was there . . .
but in the midst of snow fogs
out of which the sun rises
showing the variorum of fate
as others look up at the sky
beseeching the creator
to carpenter their dreams.

Wither peace?

They dance in the dark alleys
and feast with friends in fury
blood and water on their lips.
Their songs are of rolling wave
the music echoes of thunder
Where shall be peace?

Peace, peace we seek
mankind's lost treasure
present through the lights of faith
erected on words and ways
as souls and minds confess
there should be peace.

In sunny weather and rainfall
they kneel at altars unknown
to the temples of conscience
from souls joined in chains
but peace we seek.

They roam around by day
and plunge at nightfall.
Thoughts spread like ocean's tide
struggling with body and soul
to inherit the earth.
May peace reign!

The coming peace

Hand-in-hand we'll team
& march along harm's way
to avoid harm
shuttling between the known
and the perceived.

We'll shoot at weightless pyramids
of missiles and graceless Generals
and shut off their fountains
from watering the seeds
of death.

Our barrels will roll
from dusk till dawn
and rattle through night-winds
since this darkness that shields liberty
must fall in our struggle for peace.

The peace will surely come
through thick and thin.
It shall manifest a new destiny
for a bruised and bleeding nation
freed from the grip of banditry.

Tranformation and Change

Contents of our season

We wander and wonder
with thoughts stored in apparition
as we search for the moon
when the sun is needed
to dry up our soaked crops.

Our deserts are fast approaching
the thick terrain of our orchards and forests
moving fast along open lanes
creating void and breaking firmly
the boundaries of our groves.

The dry days are forever increasing
with aeonian frightfulness
deciduating and suffocating our hopes
abandoned by the rains
in their flight of betrayal.

The drought in its closeness
blows and is blown by winds
once stilled in expectation
qualis ab incepto
blowing over gales for storms.

The competition

This is the open competition.
It began yesterday. It continues today
at the open stadium where
their choice of tracks was open-ended
and ours was ciphered.

Every eye on the accolade.
All ears for the tattoo
hearts and hopes snuggle
for the gift and glory
of a fulgid world on sale.

"On your marks, set . . . go!" We jittered forward
trailing the loins of history. Up and down
into the shuttle of infirm foliation. Impaired. Consumed
as though thrown into the Simoon . . . but
we've been running on heated mire!

Left, Right . . . Le . . . the competition continues: dogs chasing
their tails.
unsheathed envy over clustered allures; stupefying
like the struggle between "town" and "gown"
off into the offside their team was beckoned. Ours was left
in the lurch. Glimpses of deserted lanes.

Who will zoom over the diadem . . . the prize
that carries the inveigling sign? who will
retrieve the buried hope? where is our cocalus? but keep
running; skip from these scarps of flame. Run into
the sure pocket of security.

In the interim

As I read the newspapers
I dismissed the news.
Those inventors at it again?
Creating mountains out of a void?

As I listened to the radio
I wondered why the hallucination
and the nightmare persisted
threatening twilight at down.

As I watched the television
I woke from my dream
and saw the nation zooming
fast into the orbit of 4-1-9.

A song of interim

For him who lies
in the interim
loafing lonely in rocky valleys
filled with friends lying
with cold smiles whispering
about icy wells
of deep despair.

For him who sits
Upon a long rope
against a thick wall
from whence they push
hurry, scurry and shove
past meadows and stars
in silence and haste.

For him who sings
Sour songs to sullen sounds
As sunken cathedrals ring
their melancholy bells
to brighten the embrace
of Generals whose handshakes
go beyond the elbow.

For him who sleeps
while walking in daylight
stirred by base sciolism
to the glitch of nation's quiddity
but onward his match
to the court of Rhadamanthus
traitor to his eponym.

The new generation

For them is the kingdom
structured before birth
and by birth and eched afflictions
the potions in their dark alleys.

Brought up in delicate fettle
into cubicles of human zoos
with heats that burn life's trees
good only for bats to dart.

Cluttering with toting thoughts
they roam nettled with notions of sealed gates
closed doors and consumed menu
at parties that had long been over.

No apologies yet for them at the border
of mental aberrations taking roads
toward themselves on slippery paths where
their blood whispers to their souls.

They stand so short
yet tall in their heights
their visions in reflex they call
for lights from unseen stars.

The early wounds mentholated
with solace in doubtful afflatus
they move to the ring anxious
to ride the crest of the wave.

As we welcome a change

At the flaming campaigns
they worried and warned:
wait not for their flying lies!

And they responded:
Hurry up for their promised haven.
We will trade and gain
with a changed template
on the altar of humility
within the hustles and bustles
at the vanity square market.

Wake up . . . wake up
to the challenges of change.
The game changers at work
causing laughter across the savannah.
The agents of change are agog
blowing hot and cold awaiting
a subsidized compromise!

They ride recklessly to thrill
a stiff cliff to climb
on the wings of change
to land on wheels of transformation.

A mixed bag of wealth and waste
in the winds and whirlwinds
of staggering debt portfolios
secured by celebrated transformers
and "born-again" changers.
For all treasury compromisers
and patrons of failed banks:
will change manifest the manifesto?

All hail the change
the unbroken cycle of veterans.
With the baton of hope passed
carrying the burden of expectations
with the baggage of measured adulation
flashing images of serial subsidies
whopping waivers and secreted scams
may there be light at the end
of the dark and murky tunnel
and change the changers' mined routes!

A race of beasts

The race was to a weathered sea
during a shortened rainy season.
Suddenly the river was running dry
with the boat turning
in tune with the tide.

But we all saw it coming:
The fog was heavy
Over a risen wind
below a cloudy sky
whose promise of rain was rage.

The tall trees were bowing
to the whimpering wind of the West
some wild deers bursting
into the arena of beasts
searching for a revolving catafalque

A costly movement

A savage walk in relay
through the land
left flora and fauna
seeds and seedlings mashed
under the yoke
of fast moving steps
of parasitic pilgrims.

The first round was silent
unheard among the bushes.
The second was a jugglers' jaunt
and the third a jolly jog
enervating for its stressful turn
leading to the forth round:
a ramble and a stampede!

The change of transformers

From high tension
the voltage was lowered
and the product cycle moved
up and down the plateau
to the hill of suspense.

Here come some apostles of change
fair-weather advocates of fabled reforms.
Snow will fall in the desert
and there will be harvest of gold from our rivers
but where are the fishes of yesterday?

No more bleeding but rebuilding
with blocks moulded from minerals.
But when shall we truly begin:
dredge the river of the mind
and open up the treasure store of transformation?

The change through change I, II & III

I

Echoes
Echoes of yesterday
remind the ego of dreams:
of dreams **BIG** & small
   and
of dreams small & **BIG**.

Reminders of dated smiles,
offerings and hopes
of flighty sparrows & flocking symbioses
exchanging fulminic toasts.

Echoes that bring memories
of nibbles subduing the throat . . .
of smirks for sooths.
Befunddilings . . . Soft words
and of not so soft passages
(into the garage of history).

But those echoes of yesterday
  (wrapped chasms for burial)
never said farewell.

II

The interlude
I heard the nation's bells ring
and some cages are broken;
and from the nationals a question:
ARE THESE BLESSINGS?

Wild waters are poured into roaring . . . rumbling
     yet motionless
     pounds
A siesta? Agger
or Agenesis?
"Patriotism –
     the last refuge of a scoundrel"?

III

Voices

Voices of tomorrow clothed
untried in robes of awe.
Through fouled air and crowded conclave
voices saturate messages
of fate. No longer the voices
of the weathermen:
     They predicted heavy rainfall for last week . . .
     today, the weather record attests
     we haven't had rain since yesteryears.
     Yesterday they warned against getting cold . . .
     the humidity was highest in remember'd years.

It may never rain again

Downpours have been falling
steadily in torrents
with the panting breath of thunder and lightning
beating back the dry parching breeze
moving seaward from the desert
since the peep of day.

The reigning dust is finally buried
fully and in solemn ecstatic
in earth's uterus.
our soil joys at the gain
of strength. Seedlings salute
the assurance of growth.

The naiads of our springs and rivers
toast and hail the heavy flow . . .
the drippy trickling-
all from the sky;
while the brimming wells announce
our victory over thirst.

But our eyes too may become skies
from which drops will flow
if for the lyric of this season
we overlook the path
the cyclic path
of the season's torrents.

Qualms

Vanishing visions!

Behind the veil of living
  I dream dreams
  realize realities.

I listen to many voices
   heard but a few
   with feisty fervour.

Images in the mirror:
   men without land &
    land without men.

   Men on the rough sea are sailing shoreward
     some captains are jumping ship . . .
    will others finally anchor?

  Qualms . . .

Down memory lane

We strolled charily
down memory lane
the roan river around our old town
of unrewarded solons
still stretches beyond sight.
Some of the exiled fishes are now back
but not the frogs. they are gone . . .
gone in the direction of the tiny wharves
which line the shores of our town.

We gazed over the hollows below
in the direction of the birds
flocking in speechless fear
We bawled, we laughed.
We stethoscoped the air
and listened to the sound of creation
from the infinite sky.
We fastened our lips and heard
the silence of unmapped lands.

We sped past untended cattles
rambling sheep and wide-eyed dogs
moving in crowds adrift
along the path of drowned death-dealers.
Our backs against the movement of clouds.
Against the starless night
of the dominion of almoners
nurtured by the caudle and cadging
of pirate princes.

Let's celebrate our saunter
down the valley past the baobab.
The boats are again sailing our little river.

Let's arm our souls and smooth the ruffled air
polluted by the dregs and smell
of short-winged birds.
Let's chant the forgotten apophthegms
as once again we stroll and roam
down memory lane.

Apropos of faith

Nigeria our fatherland

A beautiful land of paradox.
Domain of dreams the terrain of promise.
Pulses beat with nuts to crack
and many mountains to tear
as we build Our Fatherland.

A wonder to behold and mold
from the slow breeze of the lagoon
to the high winds of the sahara
our hopes in oneness loop to guard
Nigeria Our Fatherland.

Why these teaming masses
and empty factories
with blissful and romping rulers
watering stones leaving gardens to dry up
growing revenue leakages that yield fiscal indiscipline?

O land of ceaseless pain
where old wines get readily packaged
into new bottles
while the cities celebrate gridlocks
fueling joyless living and dying!

The soldier

He comes with songs
and drums ushering us
to a dance.

So massive in our presence
so distant from our sight
so deep in our fears.

Soon came the cannons
and the screams
the whine of flying bullets.

The heat of his battle
the smoke of the bombing
our lots manifolding.

The market

Carved to seek and salt
all from entrances and exits
the stage open night and day
in sunshine and rain
knowing no winter, spring
the harmattan and the rains
as Ananias and nymphs come and go.

They come in turns
disregarding the seasons
the sermons of solons
and go in cloud puffs
ungauged winds
and in *tohu-bohu*
courting *katabasis* and waterloo.

They come with sounds
in guttural monotones
to the sounds of feet
smiles forced or fixed
from messengers
without a message
canny and whimsy
for sisyphean simony.

Justice in the land

Our land is vast
and so is our justice:
Vast justice for a vastland.

Our land lies await
and so is our justice
vastland awaiting illimitable justice.

From the ocean to the desert
day and night: at work and play
our land is vast for justice.

Seven stories tell the tale
of justice in our land
where justice is just but just.

There was the rainbow and the sky
on which the clouds took full position
yet the rains broke out of jail.

Some drenched chicks lay fresh eggs
while the Chiefs in their shelters chirm
and chicken out with the chefs.

We cooked the eggs with oil.
But they were promptly seasoned with galls
produced by compatriots.

Then came the whirlwind
bringing desert and ocean to each other
forcing many indoors.

The folks indoors are awashed
with heavy intake of palmwine
the tappers remain locked out.

The winds blow unend
and birds sing and ask:
Is justice in the winds?

II

The rich detains the hand of justice
The poor laments the denial of justice
in a land of law and disorder
where justice is priced.

In unity

South, down South
across our wings
to the North, up North
athwart our wales
in oneness we're clogged
in unity we're geared.

Our voices shout it
our hands wave it
the legs demand a run
for oneness and unity
kept afloat and lubric
by what minds and hearts?

From the classrooms
to the Boardrooms
in unity we are parted:
East is not West
and South is not North
So is unity ice on fire?

Abuja

We arrived Abuja
dreaming dreams
and landed in a dreamland
that mirrors the mirrors
of our land and landlessness.

The roads are wide
carriers of our pride
and prejudices that flourish
in bottled conveyors
with clans frolicking and frisking.

Inside and outside of shops
and shelters converge
Conmen and Conferees enquiring
what mode of union:
for all or a portion thereof?

Whose land?
Theirs not ours
Ours not theirs . . .
Our dream mirrors illusions
transporting yesterday to tomorrow.

Abuja's trap

A net of timeless value
is woven of reports
and decrees
signed to soothe and serve
Nigeria and Nigerians.

Then came the bat
in fury and rage
turning the net sideways
to catch the animals
and leave out the birds.

Abuja's teasing

Please show me:
Show me the masterplan where
Garki breathes on Wuse and
greens are gone in Gwagwalada.

Abuja is the city we got
Abuja is the city we lost.

Abuja's promise is golden
Abuja's practice is grounding.

What makes Abuja
tempting but trouncing?
teasing with treasures tossed?
Tell me before the troops are trouped.

Abuja's treasure

Our cities lied
and they lie
Will this lie again?
Will Abuja lie?

The new-born city
is fresh and agile
boisterous and bountiful
the haven of treasures

The Gurara and Yankari –
nature's gifts and games.
Usman and Zuma join
to provide views and visions.

The centrepoint of tomorrow
of solace and strength
that prides in being the pride
of each and all?

Abuja cloud

They trampled the land
as they came
and the land vibrated
as they clapped their hands
raised up to the sky
swarthy on the southern end
sorrel at the centre
fuscous eastwards
adust northwards
cyaneous on the western end.

Is this the cloudy sky?
Abuja's blue is yielding blues
tyrian and violescent
by mid-day and viridian
berylline and grizzly before dusk.
Then aggregation of particles
in suspense and cooled
below the dew point
condensing into droplets
on Abuja's microscopic particles.

The tornado

We were firmly settled.

Mother earth was free and formed
beaming forth rays and rustling.

We scraped earth from earth
and dug with fun and pleasure
with plough and hoe in rhythm.

Thanatos was asleep
we thought and called
on *Enki* for lights through
dark farms of vampires.

The rains came stormy
over windy farms
and the tide turned polluting
streams that watered the farms
leaving us barren children
of the fruitful night.

June 12: I

The maternity of many births
dawn of a long night
of hopes and fears
of a dusk pregnant
unritualized by faith.

The child exhausts
the ingenuity of change
promotes unified unbelief
contracting social contracts
in the passage of time and hope.

Then the feasts . . .
of a season of discontent
when faith frets
yet frolic!

June 12: II

Is it nature alone that smiles
at the union of freedom and equality
in human utopias?

How about a brief spot
set to choke and free
with fumes and heat
as the smiling sun slips off!

Ahaa . . . a drop of ointment
heated on and on on all
our grief and pain.
The chromosomes of the handicapped.
The wires of a shocking embrace.

June 12: III

The matrix is shelter. An abode
sustained by rivers, lakes, ponds.
Oases of faith
attracting settlers to their shores.
Fishes, frogs, fauna emerge.
It's time to feed and feast.
The frogs around the pond worry
that mouths outruin the food
but all in shields have come
to bank and cool our river
of fire by a million restraints.

June 12: IV

Around us a mountain rises
    and falls
to ovusating forces
    of rhythm and erosion
as the rivers that swell and flood
change their courses, dry up.
River valleys turn deserts: isthmuses straits.
But can these be dreams?
The rivers flow on to settle
sediments pouring onto salty routes.

Another ship, another course.
Rickety and destination unknown
the ship keeps afloat
    on stormy waters.

We see farther than from close range:
    the sail is with bounds
      the sea is with a bottom
      somewhere lies the harbour for shelter
      and floor for anchorage.

The wailing walls

Our Nehemiah is abroad
seeking Artaxerxes
for men and materials
to rebuild our walls.

The outer gates have been broken
the inner beams gutted
by fires of our festivals
focused far from the fumes.

Nehemiah will force and fix
against Sanballat and Geshem
armed by the Tobiahs
awaiting a raid and ruin.

I missed the day

I missed the day
the day I long dreamt of
the Black's potency to show
the transience of brute to prove
I missed the day!

I missed the day
but remained unbelieving
in time's wide and fleeting range
as the struggle of life is crowned
and I missed the day.

I missed the day
as I tuned on the radio
and the armoured television of Nigeria
desolation unfurled
I missed the day.

I missed the day
as Nigeria's electronic media
chilled yet fiery gust of farce
tuned Nigeria and Nigerians away
from messages smoking out of Azania.

I missed the day
as the network news
tucked away the news of the century
into its thirteenth hour
as immunization against infection.

I missed the day
Nkosikeleli Africa . . .
And when is Nigeria to testify
to the grinning of mother Africa?
I missed the day.

Grace unlimited

We came creeping
into darkness unlimited
by our unknowing
whence we'd come
and whither heading.

The foibles unfold
daily drifting cloudlike
gliding beelike beyond the chambers
of reasoning and reckoning
aloft into a surrender.

The frightening plagues flowered
and suddenly *deus ex machina*
the vindicator of faith
turning the red lights
into green always.

The heights
(For the Heights Club, Ibadan)

The search for a sanctum
the bond of brotherhood
tied by tissues of faith
kept all coming.

The Heights was the vision
love its seed
planted in mind and movement
of each and all.

Aloft to the heights the lift
of men and spouses
and siblings in unison
no height beyond reach.

We climb the rising slope
with each passing day
sowing grains and watering
soils for the Heights.

Between sunrise and sunset
Our sinews from the Almighty sprout
as we camp and cultivate
the heights for the Heights.

Today is for tomorrow
(*For my grandchildren*)

You are my future –
a legacy that works
perfectly on God's own promise
the outcome of my dreams.

My today is for your tomorrow
given in sweat and sacrifice
for your mind, soul and inspiration
as I sing and beat the drums.

Ben Franklin, the poet had warned:
"One day, today is worth two tomorrows"
for a duty dodged is tomorrow's debt
since daylight will fade for evening's sake.

When procrastination visits
we were told by forebears
it comes to steal our time
but it is the thief of destinies.

A legacy strong to climb
the ladder of prosperity
for the pains of today faced
the pleasure of tomorrow sealed.

To tomorrow do I vow
pledging hope and flying
the flag of optimism
How bright your colours will glow!

The covenants, I, II & III

I
Covenant with the road

In the morning I will
rise and race for life's desires
I will ring bells for rallies
at noon and set raceways
for nights' chosen Romeos.

In the morning I will
go east and turn
westwards within the range
across the northern borders steering
beyond my southern imagination.

I will go left and turn
right at mornings, day and night
in sunshine or rain I will
foot, ride or drive
checking in and out of solitude.

I will go unhurt
and return without a hitch
slowly or with speed fulfilling
the unbroken, sacred and eternal
covenant with the road.

II
Covenant with fate

How should it be said:
with lyric and songs or whistles
that the accord with fate
is sealed in the canal of life?

I hold forth the testament
attesting to tyrannies and terror
the flowage of unwanted waters
from the sea's swelling pocket.

I am caged within four walls
looking through the window and seeing
the heat scalding through the sun
with birds looking for trees to share.

It's rain today and sun tomorrow
the sheep and the shepherd confounded
gazing over landscapes with tall lean trees
as the streams run dry.

The lights are off
and all is darkness yet
the usurpers' fires continue to burn cities
covered in sheets of puffing clouds.

Their forebears once were
in their dank and dark castles
in homes and hevels of infamy
celebrating the captivity of the defenceless.

The captives' souls are bleeding.
They tremble in agony.
Their hands in chains.

The stomachs are tied and tried.

I watch them in their wrecks
victims of the festival of baboons
armoured against unwelcomed fate.
I take my turn in the ring.

The sun is set to rise.
The trees in their timely spring.
The volcano has come exploding
cheering over weak cappings.

I remain with fate unbending
saying it with songs and music
celebrating the *tours de force*
now and forevermore!

III
Covenant with him

This final covenant
is with Him
the First and the Last.

He commands and causes
to begin and end:
"You may ask me for anything
in my name
and I will do it"
assures His son.

"I am the way,
the truth
and the life"
He confirms.

Follow me then for His promise.
Come on to the Calvary
through the rivers of life
herebefore and hereafter.

Hallowed be the Commander
of my ship through storms
my battle in the jungle
of mines and mammons.
With triumph assured
find me wholly by His feet.

Appendix

THE ESSENCE OF POLITICAL POETRY

(Being the speech made by the author during the Presentation of **Fate Unearthed** *at Draper's Hall, Institute of African Studies, University of Ibadan on Wednesday 01 June, 1983)*

The various schools of thought on creative writing are so well known that we need not waste time reviewing them. Each writer, young or old, belongs to one "School" or the other. As for me, I do not write for the fun of it. It is not a mere occasional pastime. I write to convey a message – and that message is, in most cases, political.

Last night, as I sat reflecting upon what to say today, some thoughts kept crossing my mind. The first was on the need (and how best) to take poetry back to the people and for the people to accept poetry once again. The second was on the pretensions that have invaded the craft over the years. The third was on why I even bother to write poetry!

The works of Shakespeare, Dante, Yeats, Virgil, Keats, Frost, Dickinson, Pope, the Metaphysicals, the Coevals (especially Donne and Eliot) and others like Neruda, Baraka, Giovanni, Okigbo, Soyinka, Awoonor, Clark-Bekederemo, etc, are very much in circulation. Why new poetry? Why don't we continue to reproduce them for future circulation? Will that really make any difference to future generations? Have they made the intended or anticipated impacts on our own world and lives?

We, however, have entered a bitter and bewildering age in which we must respond to the weather of new times. Poetry, to me, should be one of the weapons with which to respond. But it must be employed beyond buttressing the

Heraclitean *"reality of change"*. We must search to illuminate, inspire and change a world system and individual existence whose paradox and passions are painfully evident under the burden of daily struggle.

How do we take poetry back to the people and how do we make them accept it? The answer seems intuitively obvious – but by no means revealed like an object before the searching eyes. We have to go back into history: to Ezra Pound (although very often in support of a wrong cause) in his time, to Pablo Neruda, to Chris Okigbo in his days, the Mbari era, etc. Saint Augustine knew so much about the imperfections of the city on earth and turned to the heavenly city–but not Machiavelli who saw it as wanting but reparable. And while his *The Prince* is parochial and statist, his *Discorsi* in which Romulus is defended for killing Remus for the common good is no less universal than Kant's deontological imperative of morality. Hegel takes off from here, relating moral standard to social relations. Many others looked elsewhere and were lost to history.

In our time, not many are showing interest in philosophical and literary works, especially poetry, ostensibly because people are not that interested any more. We never cared to probe why people loved poetry in the past and now seem to abhor it. Part of the problem revolves around the issue of relevance. Today, the nation's soul is on fire. There is hunger and misery, criminal corruption and bare-faced tyranny. There is structural and social decadence. People are being misruled by gangs of parasites and predators without the slightest regard for humanity and the rule of law. And we are presently rolling along a circular course of systemic disarray. Yet many of our writers continue to romanticize the past. They, including the neoteric, write as if they are in a different world! With that, nobody would take poetry seriously. It has to be relevant for it to be accepted. And continuous interest and acceptability could be anchored only to poetry's tissue of relevance.

I believe that poetry could be taken back to the people through the classrooms, workshops, associations/societies and the mass media. I also believe that it would be accepted so long as it is relevant. Poetry should be used to echo the cries of those suffering from hunger, social alienation, economic oppression or political tyranny. It would be accepted so long there are no pretensions; as long as the writers are objective with a liberating vision, crafting faithful reproductions of reality, and do not play God the Father.

Now, I have to move on straight away to why I bother to write poetry since I have a heavy burden in my own discipline. Some of us who grew up in the literary world of the sixties anxiously awaited a re-orientation, a re-awakening of literary interest and a shifting of our mental horizon. Soyinka, Okigbo and Baraka were stimulating forebears – followed by Awoonor, Sonia Sanchez, Kalu Uka, etc. –people with intense feelings and imaginative grasp of their societies. In the seventies we noticed a literary recession or, put differently, did not see the type of literary upsurge that ought to have accompanied the development in our immediate and external environment.

The more one looked to see people take up the challenge the less one saw, and one became more convinced that we should be part of the answer. There was, of course, the constant reminder to be found on page 106 of Rene Wellek and Austin Warren's **The Theory of Literature (New York 1942)** that *". . .literature is no substitute for Sociology or Politics. It has its own justification and aim. "*But what on earth prevents a creator from growing beyond an "ordinary artist" into being a real thinker, a dialectician, even an ideologue or a didactician? The frontiers of art are deep and wide. This would explain why Plato equated the study of art with the study of moral values and Aristotle equated art with poetic values and the study of aesthetics. To us, the values of art – especially poetry – interact and blend with moral, economic, historical and political values. In short poetry represents, in the words of Charles Augustin Sainte-Beuve, "an invitation to action."

While one could, through political analysis, engineer the movement of humanity forward toward the ideal, toward perfection, poetry has the power (in the ancient Hellenic sense) of helping to form the normative consciousness which, within the context of contemporary societies, would reinforce the ideal. Indeed, it is our belief that poetry could be used effectively like Zeno's arrow and, with it, reach the heart of man and discharge the fluids of liberation and upliftment.

Finally, since *Fate Unearthed* is being presented today, I believe that a word on the collection, beyond what is contained in the "preface", is quite in order. I no doubt anticipate critical incomprehension of *Fate Unearthed*. But, in fairness to those who might have genuine axe to grind, I have to reiterate three views which have influenced some of the collection:

i.   The absurdities in our world must be faced and fought, the world and its peoples do not deserve to be merely contemplated with tolerant pity, their pasts romanticized or their present misery rationalized.

ii.   While the organisation of a poem in metre and rhyme has its own basic advantages, efforts should be made from time to time to devise new forms and genres to make a work really creative without, at the onset, planting seeds which could grow into oaks or confusion.

iii. Poetry should forever remain an important weapon for sharpening human sensibilities and for making man truly human.

114

And so we shall continue
to use poetry our searchlight
in muddy rivers of dark waters
in the thick jungle of raving deamons
lest drowned we become
in the confluence
or lost we remain
in the depths.

Kraftgriots

Also in the series (POETRY) *continued*

Ebi Yeibo: *Maiden Lines* (2004)
Barine Ngaage: *Rhythms of Crisis* (2004)
Funso Aiyejina: *I, The Supreme & Other Poems* (2004)
'Lere Oladitan: *Boolekaja: Lagos Poems 1* (2005)
Seyi Adigun: *Bard on the Shore* (2005)
Famous Dakolo: *A Letter to Flora* (2005)
Olawale Durojaiye: *An African Night* (2005)
g'ebinyŏ ogbowei: *let the honey run & other poems* (2005)
Joe Ushie: *Popular Stand & Other Poems* (2005)
Gbemisola Adeoti: *Naked Soles* (2005)
Aj. Dagga Tolar: *This Country is not a Poem* (2005)
Tunde Adeniran: *Labyrinthine Ways* (2006)
Sophia Obi: *Tears in a Basket* (2006)
Tonyo Biriabebe: *Undercurrents* (2006)
Ademola O. Dasylva: *Songs of Odamolugbe* (2006), winner, 2006 ANA/Cadbury
    poetry prize
George Ehusani: *Flames of Truth* (2006)
Abubakar Gimba: *This Land of Ours* (2006)
G. 'Ebinyo Ogbowei: *the heedless ballot box* (2006)
Hyginus Ekwuazi: *Love Apart* (2006), winner, 2007 ANA/NDDC Gabriel Okara
    poetry prize and winner, 2007 ANA/Cadbury poetry prize
Abubakar Gimba: *Inner Rumblings* (2006)
Albert Otto: *Letters from the Earth* (2007)
Aj. Dagga Tolar: *Darkwaters Drunkard* (2007)
Idris Okpanachi: *The Eaters of the Living* (2007), winner, 2008 ANA/Cadbury
    poetry prize
Tubal-Cain: *Mystery in Our Stream* (2007), winner, 2006 ANA/NDDC Gabriel
    Okara poetry prize
John Iwuh: *Ashes & Daydreams* (2007)
Sola Owonibi: *Chants to the Ancestors* (2007)
Adewale Aderinale: *The Authentic* (2007)
Ebi Yeibo: *The Forbidden Tongue* (2007)
Doutimi Kpakiama: *Salute to our Mangrove Giants* (2008)
Halima M. Usman: *Spellbound* (2008)
Hyginus Ekwuazi: *Dawn Into Moonlight: All Around Me Dawning* (2008), winner,
    2008 ANA/NDDC Gabriel Okara poetry prize
Ismail Bala Garba & Abdullahi Ismaila (eds.): *Pyramids: An Anthology of Poems
    from Northern Nigeria* (2008)
Denja Abdullahi: *Abuja Nunyi (This is Abuja)* (2008)
Japhet Adeneye: *Poems for Teenagers* (2008)
Seyi Hodonu: *A Tale of Two in Time (Letters to Susan)* (2008)
Ibukun Babarinde: *Running Splash of Rust and Gold* (2008)
Chris Ngozi Nkoro: *Trails of a Distance* (2008)

Tunde Adeniran: *Beyond Finalities* (2008)
Abba Abdulkareem: *A Bard's Balderdash* (2008)
Ifeanyi D. Ogbonnaya: *... And Pigs Shall Become House Cleaners* (2008)
g'ebinyŏ ogbowei: *the town crier's song* (2009)
g'ebinyŏ ogbowei: *song of a dying river* (2009)
Sophia Obi-Apoko: *Floating Snags* (2009)
Akachi Adimora-Ezeigbo: *Heart Songs* (2009), winner, 2009 ANA/Cadbury poetry prize
Hyginus Ekwuazi: *The Monkey's Eyes* (2009)
Seyi Adigun: *Prayer for the Mwalimu* (2009)
Faith A. Brown: *Endless Season* (2009)
B.M. Dzukogi: *Midnight Lamp* (2009)
B.M. Dzukogi: *These Last Tears* (2009)
Chimezie Ezechukwu: *The Nightingale* (2009)
Ummi Kaltume Abdullahi: *Tiny Fingers* (2009)
Ismaila Bala & Ahmed Maiwada (eds.): *Fireflies: An Anthology of New Nigerian Poetry* (2009)
Eugenia Abu: *Don't Look at Me Like That* (2009)
Data Osa Don-Pedro: *You Are Gold and Other Poems* (2009)
Sam Omatseye: *Mandela's Bones and Other Poems* (2009)
Sam Omatseye: *Dear Baby Ramatu* (2009)
C.O. Iyimoga: *Fragments in the Air* (2010)
Bose Ayeni-Tsevende: *Streams* (2010)
Seyi Hodonu: *Songs from My Mother's Heart (2010),* winner ANA/NDDC Gabriel Okara poetry prize, 2010
Akachi Adimora-Ezeigbo: *Waiting for Dawn* (2010)
Hyginus Ekwuazi: *That Other Country* (2010), winner, ANA/Cadbury poetry prize, 2010
Emmanuel Frank-Opigo: *Masks and Facades* (2010)
Tosin Otitoju: *Comrade* (2010)
Arnold Udoka: *Poems Across Borders* (2010)
Arnold Udoka: *The Gods Are So Silent & Other Poems* (2010)
Abubakar Othman: *The Passions of Cupid* (2010)
Okinba Launko: *Dream-Seeker on Divining Chain* (2010)
'kufre ekanem: *the ant eaters* (2010)
McNezer Fasehun: *Ever Had a Dear Sister* (2010)
Baba S. Umar: *A Portrait of My People* (2010)
Gimba Kakanda: *Safari Pants* (2010)
Sam Omatseye: *Lion Wind & Other Poems* (2011)
Ify Omalicha: *Now that Dreams are Born* (2011)
Karo Okokoh: *Souls of a Troubadour* (2011)
Ada Onyebuenyi, Chris Ngozi Nkoro, Ebere Chukwu (eds): *Uto Nka: An Anthology of Literature for Fresh Voices* (2011)
Mabel Osakwe: *Desert Songs of Bloom* (2011)
Pious Okoro: *Vultures of Fortune & Other Poems* (2011)
Godwin Yina: *Clouds of Sorrows* (2011)
Nnimmo Bassey: *I Will Not Dance to Your Beat* (2011)
Denja Abdullahi: *A Thousand Years of Thirst* (2011)
Enoch Ojotisa: *Commoner's Speech* (2011)
Rowland Timi Kpakiama: *Bees and Beetles* (2011)

117

Lawrence Ogbo Ugwuanyi: *Let Them Not Run* (2011)
Saddiq M. Dzukogi: *Canvas* (2011)
Arnold Udoka: *Running with My Rivers* (2011)
Olusanya Bamidele: *Erased Without a Trace* (2011)
Olufolake Jegede: *Treasure Pods* (2012)
Karo Okokoh: *Songs of a Griot* (2012), winner. ANA/NDDC Gabriel Okara
    poetry prize, 2012
Musa Idris Okpanachi: *From the Margins of Paradise* (2012)
John Martins Agba: *The Fiend and Other Poems* (2012)
Sunnie Ododo: *Broken Pitchers* (2012)
'Kunmi Adeoti: *Epileptic City* (2012)
Ibiwari Ikiriko: *Oily Tears of the Delta* (2012)
Bala Dalhatu: *Moonlights* (2012)
Karo Okokoh: *Manna for the Mind* (2012)
Chika O. Agbo: *The Fury of the Gods* (2012)
Emmanuel C. S. Ojukwu: *Beneath the Sagging Roof* (2012)
Amirikpa Oyigbenu: *Cascades and Flakes* (2012)
Ebi Yeibo: *Shadows of the Setting Sun* (2012)
Chikaoha Agoha: *Shreds of Thunder* (2012)
Mark Okorie: *Terror Verses* (2012)
Clemmy Igwebike-Ossi: *Daisies in the Desert* (2012)
Idris Amali: *Back Again (At the Foothills of Greed)* (2012)
A.N. Akwanya: *Visitant on Tiptoe* (2012)
Akachi Adimora-Ezeigbo: *Dancing Masks* (2013)
Chinazo-Bertrand Okeomah: *Furnace of Passion* (2013)
g'ebinyö ogbowei: *marsh boy and other poems* (2013)
Ifeoma Chinwuba: *African Romance* (2013)
Remi Raji: *Sea of my Mind* (2013)
Francis Odinya: *Never Cry Again in Babylon* (2013)
Immanuel Unekwuojo Ogu: *Musings of a Pilgrim* (2013)
Khabyr Fasasi: *Tongues of Warning* (2013)
J.C.P. Christopher: *Salient Whispers* (2014)
Paul T. Liam: *Saint Sha'ade and other poems* (2014)
Joy Nwiyi: *Burning Bottom* (2014)
R. Adebayo Lawal: *Melodreams* (2014)
R. Adebayo Lawal: *Music of the Muezzin* (2014)
Idris Amali: *Efeega: War of Ants* (2014)
Samuel Onungwe: *Tantrums of a King* (2014)
Bizuum G. Yadok: *Echoes of the Plateau* (2014)
Abubakar Othman: *Bloodstreams in the Desert* (2014)
rome aboh: *a torrent of terror* (2014)
Udenta O. Udenta: *37 Seasons Before the Tornado* (2015)
Magnus Abraham-Dukuma: *Dreams from the Creek* (2015)
Christian Otobotekere: *The Sailor's Son 1* (2015)
Tanure Ojaide: *The Tale of the Harmattan* (2015)

Printed in the United States
By Bookmasters